Feeling Frustrated

by Penny Anderson
illustrated by
Dan Siculan

THE CHILD'S WORLD

ELGIN, ILLINOIS 60120

Distributed by Childrens Press, 1224 West Van Buren Street, Chicago, Illinois 60607.

Library of Congress Cataloging in Publication Data

Anderson, Penny S.
  Feeling frustrated.

  (What's in a word?)
  Rev. ed. of: Frustrated. ©1982.
  Summary: Describes a number of situations which can cause frustration, such as breaking and losing items, staying inside on a rainy day, being called names, and feeling sick.
  1. Frustration—Juvenile literature.   [1. Frustration.
2. Emotions]   I. Siculan, Dan, ill.   II. Title.
III. Series.
BF575.F7A57   1983   152.4   82-19910
ISBN 0-89565-245-5

    4 5 6 7 8 9 10 11 12 R 89 88 87

Feeling Frustrated

Frustrated—To feel disappointed;
to be unable to do what one wants;
to want to do two things and have
to choose one of them.

Today was such a bad day!
  My music box
  crashed to the floor
  when I bumped it.
  The lady's head broke off.

All day long, things went wrong.
  A ball hit me
  right in the face.
  My shoelace came untied—
  and I tripped on it.

There's a trying-not-to-cry
  hurt in my throat, now.
  Tell me, have you ever had
  such a bad day?

—Sylvia Root Tester

When accidents happen,

I GET FRUSTRATED

"Let me pour it . . .
  I can do it!"
  "You may try," she said.

When I poured,
  of course, I spilled it
    all over Jamie's head.

Mr. Northrup raises roses—
pink and yellow, white and red.
All the dirt is soft around them,
a warm and fragrant
flower bed.

Mr. Northrup watched me riding
my new, blue, two-wheeled bike.
I waved at him and ran right over
those bright roses
we both like.

All the branches and the petals
splattered, shattered in the dirt.
They were ruined, but Mr. Northrup
ran to see
if I was hurt.

I wasn't hurt. I was frustrated.
I wanted to run away and hide.
It seems as if I do something stupid
every time
I ride.

Then there are things
 I just can't do and—

I AM FRUSTRATED

"Don't hold it like that.
 Choke up on the bat!
Spread your feet apart.
 Shape up! Look smart!"

I can't EVER do
 what they tell me to—
keep my eye on the ball,
 swing hard and not fall!

"Emily Ann's a scaredy-cat.
Emily Ann's afraid. . . ."

I climbed it once
and fell on my head.
I skinned my knee;
it even bled.

"Emily Ann's a scaredy-cat.
Emily Ann's afraid. . . ."
   I'll climb it again
   and probably fall—
   or maybe pretend
   I don't hear them call.

"Emily Ann's a scaredy-cat.
Emily Ann's afraid. . . ."
   Don't call me names;
   you never should.
   It frustrates me
   and I don't feel good.

   Besides, I am NOT a scaredy-cat!
   I am NOT afraid!

A hungry grey squirrel
   with a fluffy, puffy tail
   sat on our fence.
   His paws were folded
   like praying hands
across his furry chest.

I tried to paint
   a picture of him.
   I worked all during snacks
   while Timmy stuffed crackers
   in his mouth
and laughed at my mistakes.

When things go wrong,

I FEEL FRUSTRATED

Daddy said he'd take me fishing.
   He promised me we'd go
Down along the river bank
   Where the cattails grow.

Mommy said that Daddy called.
   He has to work tonight.
There's nothing to do but sit around,
   Pretending it's all right.

When I ate my soup,
    I burned my tongue.
I pinched my finger
    in the dresser drawer.
My left shoe's tied
    with the tongue outside,
and my right one
    walks all wrong.

Where is it?
  Where is it?

Where's my chocolate rabbit
I saved here in my drawer?

It's gone!
  All gone!

I saved it to take for show and tell
And to eat at recess.

Where did it go, Jeff?
  Where did it go?

YOU

    ATE

        IT?

            NO!

It's raining,
It's raining,
It's raining again.

Won't it ever stop?
Katy wants to go with me
To play on the swings
In the park.
But. . . .

It's raining,
It's raining,
It's raining again.

It's raining everywhere,
So Katy can't come play with me.
And I can't play
With her.

I want to go out and play in the snow—
　　Slide down the hill on my sled.
But I can't play out and run and shout.
　　I have to stay in bed.

My blanket's too hot. My pillows are flat.
　　My puzzle fell on the floor.
My head aches, my eyes hurt,
　　And my throat is getting sore.

But I want to go out and play in the snow—
　　Slide down the hill on my sled.
I want to play out and run and shout.
　　I don't want to stay in bed.

And too many don't's make me

FRUSTRATED

Don't run,
WALK!

Don't yell,
TALK!

Don't spill,
DRINK!

Don't forget,
THINK!

Don't smash,
FIX!

Don't bite,
KISS!

Don't hate,
LOVE!

Too many don'ts make me
FRUSTRATED!

I have some frustrating days
when everything
goes wrong.
On those days
I act mad, sad, or bad.

When I am frustrated
and nothing
is going right,
it helps to know
others understand.

I hope I understand
when others have
bad days.

About the Author:

Penny Anderson holds a degree in elementary education from Western Illinois University. A former Illinois State University faculty associate who taught language arts in the Metcalf Laboratory School, Ms. Anderson has written extensively for teachers—and for children. She and her husband now live in New Smyrna Beach, Florida.

About the Artist:

Dan Siculan studied art fundamentals at the Oglebay Institute in Wheeling, West Virginia, and life drawing at the American Academy of Art in Chicago. His career began while in the army where he served as an artist while stationed in Europe. Mr. Siculan later worked as a commercial artist, becoming free lance in 1951. He is proficient in painting in oils, acrylics, and water color media and has produced numerous editions of original serigraphs. He is married and has four children and three grandchildren.